P.E.A.K. Ways

by

Robert E. Saltmarsh

authorHOUSE™

1663 LIBERTY DRIVE, SUITE 200
BLOOMINGTON, INDIANA 47403
(800) 839-8640
WWW.AUTHORHOUSE.COM

Frontispiece

This is a manual for choice making when couple relationships begin to suffer and difficult passages become more frequent.

One assumption is that both partners intend to preserve and enhance the relationship they have formed.

"COUPLE" is defined as a two-person relationship wherein each regards the other as " SIGNIFICANT"! This would include special friendships, people who live together, people who are engaged, and people who are married to each other.

The suggestions provided in this reading may also apply to colleagues, fellow workers, neighbors, and those of you who enjoy doing "Random Acts of Kindness" occasionally as well as intentionally.

These ideas have accumulated since 1954, and have developed in design and teaching of a special course entitled "Facilitating Interpersonal Relationships" and Workshops at Miami University, Indiana University, and Eastern Illinois University.

This work is intended for all of us who have hoped that all was well and discovered that it wasn't, and didn't quite know what to do about it. Stride firmly as you find things that may make positive differences for you and the significant ones whose hopes are blended with yours.

Acknowledgements

I am indebted to each of the following for specific editing, suggestions, and inspirations carefully woven into this manuscript with sincere appreciation:

Suellyn Garner - Educator, Musician, and Gourmet Cook, for: grammar, punctuation, typos, and proper use of italics.

Kerry Lynn Smith - B.A, Advertising/Journalism, Ms. Counseling Psychology, and my daughter, for: reducing my excess wording, tightening composition and deleting psychology jargon.

Barbara Schlauch - Native German, American Citizen, Teacher of English as a second language, and observer of world cultures for: re-sequencing sections awkward for second language readers, and feasible language for the range of potential readers.

Markay Ann Saltmarsh - my wife for: Steadfast authenticity, as together, we two have learned how to extract ourselves from our own BARK cycles and use our PEAK Choices well. As of July 31, 2003 it will have been a fifty-year clinic for both

of us. She remains the indomitable Lady that I
love.

My colleagues, students and clients at Miami University,
Indiana University, and Eastern Illinois University
and in my private practice who have consistently
nudged my knowledge and skills beyond all
bumps and around all curves.

Table of Contents

Introduction - A typical BARK cycle: xiii

Chapter One: BARKING BACK or PEAKING
FORWARD Two Patterns of choice for Getting Along
Together 1
    FINE POINTS ABOUT BARKING 2
    Deleting "bark bytes" from your end of the cycle 7

Chapter Two: The PEAK Model 9
    PEEKING AT "PEAKING"................................. 10
    Entering the PEAK model; Simplest "P": 13
    The Peak Map – Basic Structure......................... 16
    Beyond Minimal Possibilities 18

Chapter Three: P"E"AK EXAMINE RESULTS 21
    Examination Standards: 23

Chapter Four: PE"A"K ACTIVATING RESOURCES .. 25
    (Doing/Watching) 27
    Thinking/Self-talk/ Switch boards: 30
    Blocks to Creativity 33
    Self-Limiting Beliefs 36
    VOWS... 46

YOUR TIMELINES 47

Chapter Five: PEA"K" <u>K</u>EEPING WHAT WORKS..... 51
    Recovering and Activating Resourceful States... 53
    Caring Deeds.. 55

Chapter Six: ADVANCED PEAKS 57
    GIVING OF SELF SKILLS 57
    TAKING (listening)... 61
    SEEKING (Asking) 63
    FEEDBACK 65

Chapter Seven: PLATFORMS FOR NEGOTIATING . 75
    1A.   Negotiating with your self 75
    100.   The BARK check list................................. 75
    Platform 101: "You – Me – Us – Proposal" 79
    Platform 102: "Principled Negotiations" 81
    Platform 103: The "Reconcilable Differences"
    Platform 86
    104.   Details about Rapport 90
    Flash points, anguish, despair. 94

Chapter Eight: DESIGNING A COMPELLING
FUTURE 97

Chapter Nine: Life Style: Eight Ideas for Building and
Enjoying Yours... 103

Reference List..117

Introduction - A typical BARK cycle:

Eugene and Thelma start a Saturday morning with high hopes.

She thinks he'll mow the yard and clean the garage. He thinks it's been a long time since making love and she'll make the first move.

Eugene waits around looking for signs of hope. Thelma waits for the garage door to open so she can start the washing machine.

Nothing happens!

He thinks "she was always ready on Saturday mornings when we first were married".

She thinks " he's got to know the grass is high and the garage is a mess. He always does these things on time".

Thelma: *I've got a busy day today.*

Eugene: *I'm not surprised, you always do.*

Thelma: *What's that supposed to mean?*

Eugene: *The hell with it. I'm going out for breakfast.*

Thelma: *Just like your Dad always did!*

Saturday's hopes are dead and Sunday may be in peril. These two have reentered their familiar BARK CYCLE. Distance is growing between them. Unless the cycle is broken with new and different attitudes and behaviors, the poisons will accumulate. What once was warm and caring will become cool and competitive.

Couples rarely need training to generate these powerful cycles of turmoil and slow withering of that which brought them together.

The first thing is to understand the cycles. The second thing is to learn about how to interrupt them and replace them with more promising patterns.

What follows intends to do both.

Chapter One:

BARKING BACK or PEAKING FORWARD

Two Patterns of choice for *Getting Along Together*

Robert E. Saltmarsh ED. D.

In Marriage, parenting, *significant other relationships,* and friendships "getting along" and how to do it are matters of chance or habit for many of us. When togetherness appears to be in for a crash landing, it is helpful to inspect what has been happening and whether or how things might be changed. The two patterns that follow are offered in the spirits of choice awareness, and hope.

The BARK Pattern:	The PEAK Pattern:
*B*ackground	*P*ick, *P*ractice, *P*resent new *P*atterns
*A*nticipation	*E*xamine Results
*R*udeness	*A*ctivate Resources
*K*nicks	*K*eep what works

The Bark pattern of interaction is an inheritance of the human condition. It develops naturally and tends to tighten with each cycle of interaction between two caring persons. Despite the rich promise of formal education which provides knowledge for how to do almost anything prior to having to do it, being a part of a couple is largely left to on the job training. Couples are left to cut their own cloth and usually rely on the patterns observed from parents, relatives, celebrities, or other concoctions formed by trial and error.

Once the early adventures of attraction and coupling have subsided, the daily dosage of amorous drama dwindles to the daily dwindle of the business of getting along together.

Soon other dramas drift to center stage. Dramas like: who is in control, who has "done wrong", who chases who, how to win, how to survive, and how to retrieve "good graces" with each other.

FINE POINTS ABOUT BARKING

Background: Each person has information about the other including where both grew up, family characteristics, imperfections, trauma survived, triumphs, etc. This becomes a matter of personality history to the other. The awareness of WHO the other one is in the moment easily disappears. The You and Me defaults in to your parents and my memory.

Anticipation: Each has become a character in the other's scenario of the on going drama. Each knows what the other is likely to think or do. Each then plays out aspects of what they predict will happen. Each then forms the counterpoints, sarcasms, and strategies to diminish the other and preserve superiority.

Rudeness: Now that each person is basically an adversary to the other, spontaneous forms of respect, courtesy, warmth, and caring are replaced with the need to win, defend, put the other in their place, or acknowledge that the other can't help it given where they came from. From the mildest forms of hidden abuse, competitive implied insults can escalate and shut off most forms of Getting Along.

Knicks: The collection of injuries from the above cycle is properly sorted by each into categories that range from mild to severe or beyond to "never again". Thus all potential loving moments become burdened with scar tissue and the young love or friendship that originally brought each to the other becomes history, seldom to fully flame again.

The tensions of the BARK Cycles are tightened still further.

Example (next Saturday):

Eugene; *I've known since you mentioned it yesterday that you would do everything possible to prevent me from buying a used car.*

Thelma: *When have we ever worked out what to do about our cars?*

Eugene: *That's just it! You will find a way to smash anything I try to do.*

Thelma: *Well I've had to suffer through too many of your harebrained schemes and I'm tired of it.*

Eugene: *That's why I never discuss things ahead of time. You'll raise all kinds of hell about it and nothing ever gets done.*

BARK cycles like this require no rehearsal and medicine does not sooth the KNICKS that accumulate to corrupt the *getting along together* ideal that should make being together better than being apart.

When enough "Bark" Cycles have been completed, the dignity of each participant as well as the dignity of the Relationship becomes frozen. The term "dignity" means: "to be worthy of honor and respect". Dignity is based on having wisdom of choice active and available. Relationships easily become locked into the BARK model and often reduce to only five choices for each individual:

1. Win.

2. Give in.

3. Pay back.

4. Tolerate.

5. Withdraw.

Combinations of numbers 2,3,4, &5 above can form the mixtures by which mischief descends upon the member who thought they'd won only to discover the victory may be hollow or have serious costs. A fresh new cycle rises: B....A...R...&...K are each reactivated with steadied expertise and enhanced commitment. People get better at this with practice!

Notice that The BARK model is made up of nouns! Nouns are names of things and only sparsely represent active, ongoing, procedures. When nouns are converted to actions, the representations become more complex. Example: "How is your relationship?" Is a bit easier to answer with one word than "How are you relating?". Verb forms tend to bring action into view. The capacity of each BARK veteran to use insulting nouns or convert them into elaborate verb forms (gerunds) which indict, inflame, or insult the other is embedded somewhere in each of the relationship tragedies that make the news.

The ground soil of the BARK structure is the cycle shown below. Once a problem emerges, It is a human reflex to place blame so it can be removed or fixed. The costs are often dreadful and lead to defensiveness, counter charges, and accumulated KNICKS.

The BARK strategies are thus renewed and new blame cycles are set in motion. Such *Merry-Go-Rounds* seldom provide brass rings for the participants.

The Blame Cycle!!

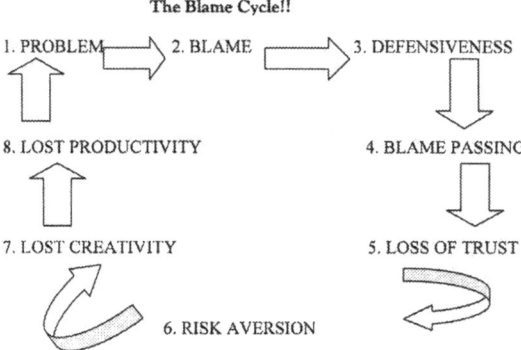

1. PROBLEM → 2. BLAME → 3. DEFENSIVENESS

8. LOST PRODUCTIVITY   4. BLAME PASSING

7. LOST CREATIVITY   5. LOSS OF TRUST

6. RISK AVERSION

You can locate your current reaction(s) at any point in the above Blame cycle. When you do, you can then interrupt the cycle and avoid the results of the rest of the cycle. If you can do this, you will have better chances to step out of your parts of the "BARKING" strategy.

Deleting "bark bytes" from your end of the cycle

Here are seven things you can choose to stop doing in order to soften the "barkiness" between the two of you. Choose at least one of them to try and if it works, add another one.

Stop glaring at your partner.

Stop swearing at your partner.

Stop yelling at your partner.

Stop asking "Why" Questions. (They require answers that justify defensiveness).

Stop solving the other person's mistakes with "helpful suggestions".

Stop making judgements about your partner's behaviors and motives.

Stop pointing your finger and accusing you partner of conduct unbecoming of a worthy person.

Soon you may have the whole menu for choosing. There may be lots more, but only you would know the things to stop that are not yet on the above list

Along the way, you may be ready to start ***doing*** <u>new things</u> instead of just deleting old ones. Then you can enter the PEAK model and discover lots of new choices for improving the ways you two get along together.

Notice that the PEAK model is made up verb forms and therefore suggest doing something different when that which you have been doing is getting toxic results.

Chapter Two:

The PEAK Model

The PEAK model is made up of options for improving the ways partners get along and by unlocking the tensions of the BARK cycles. Notice that the PEAK Model is made up of verb forms (action words) and therefore suggests doing something differently when your choices have been getting toxic results.

P: Pick new Patterns, Practice and Present them: If partners keep doing what they've always done, they'll keep getting the results they've always gotten To break the BARK cycle, at least one person must start here. Do something different!

E: Examine results: If they are better, keep doing the new things. If they are worse, at least there is a change. Try it again or change it in some way before giving up. If results are neutral, the new thing didn't meet the other person's recognition or wasn't strong enough. Repeat it or add something to it

A: Activate resources: While in the BARK cycle, your resources have been diminished. Reactivate your intelligence, creativity, vitality, maturity, eroded parts of both personalities, and revise obsolete belief systems. (See chapter four, devoted to resource activation.)

K: Keep: What works for as long as it works. Use your natural artistry to renew or elaborate the new patterns. Beware of the Tyranny of Success. New patterns used at wrong times or in wrong places may regress into new versions of the BARK cycle.

PEAK again!

PEEKING AT "PEAKING"

Even a small step out of one's own "barkhood" brings one closer to the advantages of doing things differently. Try out a few small pieces of personal dignity and be surprised when small comforts appear. Satisfaction with Self usually compares well with the evaluations imposed by a "barking" partner. Though the other may have no awareness of the change or its effects on you. Such improvements are yours to enjoy and inspire additional experiments that can lead to escape for both of you from the cycles of tension.

Here are four guidelines for "what to do when it's tense" and that can lead into the PEAK model: (Weiner-Davis,M. 1992 "Divorce Busting")

10

TAKE RESPOSIBILITY FOR EACH OF THE FOLLOWING:

1.Change first!

While it would be nice if the other person would find wisdom and begin the repair work with appropriate apology, it may be a long wait. "Mope" strategies are woefully short on stories of success, but they are still waiting. At least, pick something you know you've been doing and do its opposite. Do this for yourself – but if it happens to meet the other person's criteria it will effect both of you. This is the simplest part of the PEAK model.

2. Act as if…

The healing process is inevitable and is already underway. We have already recovered from many kinds of injuries and illnesses, and often do exactly this when new ones occur. Therefore none of us lack knowledge of how to act this way. When you get past the idea that "if you act this way the other person may think they've won" - you have at least stepped out of your part of the toxic cycle. Your healing HAS begun. This tends to diffuse the other person's BARK cycle and hope can advance.

3. Small steps are important in "Getting Along Better"!

These are the beginnings of Savings Accounts, Trips Around the world, Decent Relationships, and Trust. Any and all small changes or "caring deeds" deserve acknowledgement and appreciation. When they have been absent, welcome them within yourself and in your relationship.

4. Use the "B/F" Principle; Behavior before feelings!

Many people rely on the F/B principle (feelings first- then behavior). Under this system things get done only after the person feels like doing them. Like moping, many behaviors are still waiting to be done. Some will never be done.

Most new and different behaviors are strange and awkward. It is ugly to step out of one's habit patterns and comfort zones to do an unfamiliar behavior. That's probably why successful actors sometimes get nausea on opening night. The play goes on because the players do the behaviors anyhow! New behaviors must transcend the barriers of anger, fear, jealousy, ego, and competitiveness. BEHAVIOR well done will result in new FEELINGS more likely to be enjoyed.

There has been much said by many about "being true to one's self" and maintenance of emotional integrity. Both factors have had to be present while traveling deeper into each BARK Cycle in which the F/B system has been active and produced dogfight results.

Intention, courage, and discipline are the keys to positive change. To know that you want something different is hope.

Decide that the risks are worthy. Do what needs to be done (for yourself first and maybe for all concerned). These keys will make for movement toward Getting Along (at least better) and maybe help preserve what's important between the two of you.

Entering the PEAK model; Simplest "P":

Pick one thing that you suspect belongs in your Bark cycle and makes things worse. Then pick something to think or do that is different from that thing. At first ANYTHING is worth trying. Remember that you are entering a scientific experiment. Your interest is in finding something that will get positive change for you. Of equal interest is locating things that don't work. No need to waste efforts on things that do not get desired results!

The simplest choice is to do the opposite. If it's been loud, make it quieter. If it's been crude, make it smoother. If it's been mean, make it respectful.. Real simple things count sometimes: Change your usual posture. Alter your depth and rate of breathing. Change the habitual distance between the two of you. Move the discussion to another room or a different part of the same room. See following page(s) for extended menu.

Whatever is chosen, use the "Baseball Strategy" – 3 strikes before you're out! Since you are trying something new, you may not do it very well. The other person may not notice it or the timing may be off. So it's worth it to give the new thing at least three trials before giving up on it. (in baseball you also get 2 balls and unlimited fouls before you're out). Persistence counts, but stubbornness beyond 3 balls and maybe 4 balls may be too costly. Once you are in the PEAK model, lots of other options remain.

At worst, The simplest "P" asks for some trial and error effort rather than mindless repetition or obedience. At best, you may become The "Landlord" of your own brain patterns and their results.

Simplest "P" contiued:

PATTERNS

Pick a new and different one.

Practice it

Plan when and where to use it.

Present it (at least three times)

EXAMINE RESULTS

For you

For your partner

For the relationship – which results are useful and which are not

ACTIVATE RESOURCES

Create new Switchboards for your brain

Locate who you are and your potential

Compassion: What you care about (which of your passions are healthy and which are not)

KEEP WHAT WORKS

Refine and elaborate what you keep

Contextualize (note appropriate times, places, and situations for presenting)

Beware of the tyranny of success (if used too much, it becomes a part of a revised Bark cycle)

The Peak Map – Basic Structure

Current state:

1. Barking/Moping

2. What have been my contributions/thoughts/behaviors?

3. Stop doing each of the above.

4. Alter art least one of them. (Pick a different way of expression)

5. Do the new way at least three times.

6. Watch how your partner responds.

> Improvement? Yes! Do #'s 4 & 5 again.
>
> No! Try at least 3 times or
>
> Pick a different #4.

7. Activate your own resources of Maturity and Creativity.

Desired outcomes:

A. You can see, hear, or feel positive change in yourself or in your Partner's responses.

B. You have increased control and choice about what to do when things have gone wrong.

C. You are increasing hopes for better times.

D. You can now test new ways to get better results.

Above is the basic *what to do* structure of P.E.A.K. Ways.

BASIC "PEAKS" MENU:

Keep this page handy! Use it before things get desparate!

Change anything!

Change things that are always the same.

Change locations of where stress happens

Change times when troubles brew.

Change the one who has the choices.

Put a new step in the routine.

Reverse or re-order routines.

Predict tomorrow.   *We know if we stay the same, tomorrow will be much like today.*

If one or both of us do something different, Tomorrow may have a better chance.

Do a 180 degree turn from what you've always done.

Act "as if" the healing is already underway.

Wait or do nothing.

As last resort, do last resort.

WHEN EVEN THESE DON'T WORK:

The differences aren't different enough.

It's too soon to tell. (3 strikes before you're out!)

You're overlooking small changes in the other person.

Your heart isn't in it. Find the passion to do the new things with vitality, or wait until you do.

You've reverted to old ways. (You are "barking" again)

(Weiner-Davis, Michelle (1993) Divorce Busting: Ch.6.)

Beyond Minimal Possibilities

Partners continue in undesirable patterns because they are getting some desirable things for doing so. These things are called "secondary gains". The most obvious gains for a BARKING couple is that each is familiar with the cycle and each maintains intermittent chances for victory at the other's expense. Competition is a wonderful human experience and there are many appropriate places in our cultures for it. Apart from good games of Backgammon or Gin Rummy, marriages and committed personal relationships seldom profit with competition as an established style of "Getting Along".

When you locate the secondary gains operating in one's own cycle, you learn what you may have to give up when you change your established pattern. The Peak model can offer alternative ways to define and accomplish valuable gains without continuing the BARK cycle. When both participants gain such awareness, the habitual patterns become obsolete. It may be too much to expect that the other participant's discovery pace will be the same as yours. "PEAK'" Postulate: You are doing these choices to improve things for yourself, when they effect the other person or the way you get along, That's Gravy!

One pitfall to watch for: When you make changes in the hope that you are modeling for the other person patterns that they should imitate in how they treat you – they may not "get it". Even if they do get it, they may not do it. This is especially true when the other person is still locked in the "BARK" cycle and they have no idea that positive change may be possible.

Second pitfall: The other person may have entered their own "PEAK" Cycle and now both of you are newly introduced to one another with no familiar scripts to follow. Awkward discomforts replace the confidences of history. Poise, graceful articulation, and predictability are temporarily suspended as you meet each other in a new zone. The revised relationship must invent appropriate seasonings for the new gravy!

Poems and songs are written about the chance to start over. Good books and movies and dramatize both missed chances and new beginnings. Perhaps too much - and we every day humans leave such attractive possibilities to the artists to create fantasies to substitute for our realities. Most us did learn early on to fry our own eggs the way we want them. (There was a time when such success was thought to be impossible).

PEAK POSTULATE: Change is possible; not just a fantasy.

Robert E. Saltmarsh

Chapter Three:

"E"

EXAMINE RESULTS: Once you've stepped out of the BARK Cycle, and Picked, Practiced, and Presented something new and different, does it make a difference? For you; For the other person; For "getting along"?

Here are some differences to examine that most of us ignore:

⇒ Changes in skin color, face muscles, shoulder/chest tension, or breathing (physiology)

⇒ Changes in voice tone, volume, or tempo.(language use)

⇒ Changes in posture, position, movement, or gestures. (physical)

NOTE! These differences are evidence for you that whatever PEAK you just did has had an effect on your partner It is unwise for you to reveal or confront your partner with such observations.

Any difference at all shows that the system has been effected. Sometimes you don't even have to do it three times! Results can arrive immediately! Whooppee! Hope can expand!

Minimum Results for you:

You know the one you picked didn't work, so try it again or alter it in someway.

You know you feel better about finally doing something to improve things.

You are no longer trapped, or without choices.

Expanding choice brings expanding dignity.

Minimum Results for the other person:

They may not have noticed.....Yet !

They may be surprised.

They may not know how to respond since continued BARKING doesn't fit well.

They may think something's wrong with you or you've "gone off the deep end".

Minimum Results for "Getting Along":

The BARK cycle is interrupted for at least one of you.

There is now a chance to negotiate for better ways to be with each other.

At least one of you can be seen as who you are now, rather than what you have always been.

What is new and different may also be scary.

Examination Standards:

A. Are the results of having done something new and different better than before you peaked? YES ! You're on the right track, hang in there!

NO ! That didn't work!

a. You didn't do it very well.

b. It was poorly timed.

c. Your partner didn't notice

d. change any or all of the above and try two more times.

B. Are the results of having done something new and different worse than before you peaked?

YES! You are off-base and out of rapport with your partner and/or the situation. Ask for a break and set a time and place to talk later. Consider reading further or consulting persons you can trust. (Counselors are good at this sort of thing.)

NO! You are about even (no losses showing). Activate another resource or two and prepare for a new PEAK. Practice first to make sure it includes an element or two not in the earlier PEAK.

C. Examining Results will never go out of style. "Is it working for you?" (McGraw, 2001) remains relevant for each choice you make. Continuing as one of Freud's "civilized discontents" is no longer due to your Lot having been cast. It is due to the choices made, results examined, confirmed when useful, and changed when toxic.

Unlike Socrates we are not compelled to drink the cup of poison set before us. Even if there appears to be no other cup available, we can still choose how to respond to it. (Frankl, V 1963, *Man's Search for Meaning*).

Chapter Four:

PE"A"K

ACTIVATING RESOURCES

BRAIN WORKS
DOING/WATCHING
THINKING / SELF- TALK / SWITCH BOARDS
BLOCKS TO CREATIVITY
SELF-LIMITING BELIEFS
VOWS
YOUR TIMELINES

This section will show you the ways to get your "Best Self" operating when Tough Times are happening. Each of the above includes details you can follow to establish or regain talents or abilities that may have been ignored or gotten lost or shrunken while you have been busy "Barking Back".

When you want to PEAK, but are having a hard time, it may help to go to this "A" section as the first stop. Read and practice ones you select so you can experiment with each area or combine them when the next set of challenges comes around.

Remember the old saying: "when times are tough, the tough get going"!

PEAK Postulate: "When times are tough, the resourceful get going"!

Brain Works

When in the BARK Cycle, the latitude for "brain work" is narrow. Almost all the Barkhood is history stuff. The scenes from *BACKGROUND* are repeated in the same form time after time with only a few "spins" of self-bias added in. **ANTICIPATION** ideas become strong enough that even the surprising departures from expected patterns can be ignored or refashioned to fit in. **RUDENESS** becomes the currency of exchange.

KNICKS are tallied and saved for use as eventual justification for any of one's own failings intentional or otherwise. A typical barking cycle produces the familiar cluster of negative feelings toward your partner - and yourself! Humans hardly ever know that they can instruct their brains with choices to alter any of the above:

HOW YOUR BRAIN CAN WORK: Background (Bark) scenes arise in the brain with color, focus, size, movement, and soundtrack. Take a moment to activate one of your common ones. Pay attention to what your mind's eye/ear sees, or hears. Then ask your brain to change the color or sound of any of the characteristics. Alter in any way: if it's dark, make it light; if it's bright, make it dim;

if it's black and white, put some color in it. Do the similar changes with the sound track. Check with each experiment to determine if the results are better or worse for you. Form a better partnership with your brain to direct your brain and your relationship(s) out of the BARKS and into The PEAKS. <u>Positive Practice</u>: 1.Remember a moment when the both of you were getting along at your best. 2.Strengthen the memory by enhancing any of the colors, sounds, or meanings of that moment.

(Doing/Watching)

Changing a color is only one of many items on the "Brain Menu". Location is worth knowing about. Distance and location are easily available for our brains' events and how they form the understandings and meanings that make up our choices and what to do about them and the people about whom you care. (Andreas & Andreas, 1989, "Heart of the Mind". chs. 5,6, &7.)

Events draw us to be right inside them when they are happening. When remembering and thinking about the same events it is natural to be drawn right back inside them. All the fears, angers, passions and meanings are re-ignited and lead to "Bark- like" reactions. When one's brain has no

27

other choice(s) the joys/wounds are preserved. One becomes addicted to the joys and vengeful about the wounds.

While "inside" an event, choices are severely limited. While remembering, you can remind your brain that it is possible for you to get "outside" the event and watch it happen. Time doesn't heal everything, but it does provide distance, perspective, and choice. That's why we can learn from mistakes. We don't have to keep "barking".

We can at least start "peeking" if not "PEAKING".

You can instruct your brain to create vistas or microscopic replays of events that have happened to you. Somewhere between the two extremes are located the choices about living that will serve you well and the people about whom you care.

Disadvantaged Brain Myth: "What happened is real and always will be that way". (and so are the original reactions and meanings).

Advantaged Brain Possibilities: Memories and plans are made of colors, shapes, distances, locations, words, and sounds. Any of these, or combinations of them can be altered and re-inform understanding of what has happened. They can also help predict outcome possibilities for any creative PEAK proposals! You have a much better chance to determine which outcomes are worthwhile and which are not.

Examples:

1. Remember your last birthday, as you were doing it, by being inside those moments and notice how that feels.
2. Now remember the same events as if you are watching them from a point outside the room. Notice any differences in the intensity of how that feels.
3. Compare these two perspectives for personal meaning and potential for choosing useful beliefs and behaviors.

In example 1, you are re-doing a memory. In example 2, you both remembering and watching yourself as you choose you reactions.

PEAK POSTULATE: good and useful memories deserve RE-DOING at will.

WATCHING memories of harm can reduce pain and open potential for healthier reactions, understandings, and behavior choices.

Try similar comparisons with a few different memories of your own choice. Experiment with distances (near/far); location (up/down-right/left); sound (loud/soft-fast/slow); and color (black/white-technicolor-cloudy/clear).

Find the advantages that your brain can enjoy using to get best results for the total you.

Thinking/Self-talk/ Switch boards:

It's natural to think that "thinking" is what happens when you talk to yourself in your native word language. But Humans think faster than we make words. We think in pictures, symbols, sounds, movements, smells, tastes, touches, and emotions. Our brains can change any combination of these to form "thinkings" that yield better or worse life results. Part of the magic of being human is that we can choose how to run the switches that light up and turn on the brain. Finding the best "switch board " is part of growing up and maturing.

Different, ready-made switchboards are provided by our parents, partners, cultures, religions, jobs, schools, governments, and economies. It is easy to accept any or all of these ready-mades and live (or die) by them. The "B" of the BARK cycle is thus switched on and can remain unchallenged despite its painful results. We may need to find or create our own brand new switchboards. Some would say that this is what the notions of freedom and liberty really mean. This is where the PEAK model is useful.

Since we live in the age of psychedelics and intoxicants there is ample evidence that life altering chemical switchboards are available at certain costs and lives are indeed changed. The challenges include whether to use one's own switches or those owned by other persons or substances. The costs of the chemical and loss of autonomy are severe.

At worst, The "P" of the PEAK model asks for some trial and error effort rather than mindless repetition or obedience. At best, you may become the "Landlord" of your own Brain Patterns and their results.

Switchboard **PATTERNS**

Pick a new and different one.

Practice it.

Plan when to use it.

Present it (at least 3 times)

EXAMINE RESULTS

For you

For the other person(s)

For the relationship. (which are useful and which are not)

ACTIVATE RESOURCES

Create new Switchboard for your Brain

Locate who you are and your "mission-in –life".

Compassion-what you care about. (Which of your Passions are Healthy and which are not).

KEEP WHAT WORKS

Refine and elaborate.

Contextualize. (note appropriate times, places, and situations for Presenting)

Beware the "tyranny of success". (if used too much , it becomes a part of a revised Bark cycle)

The difference between a '"conservative" and a "liberal" is a matter of risk management: A conservative is horrified at the thought of doing something that may turn out to be wrong. A liberal is one who is horrified at the thought of missing great opportunities.

The differences between folly and legitimate risk may go back to the Garden of Eden, but those who assess them well PEAK well. Those who don't will BARK incessantly. Ever onward!

Blocks to Creativity

Fear:

By now, the two of you have customized ways to be with each other. Each of you has learned which of your abilities and extremes do not fit well into your ways of getting along together. Each has deleted, reduced, or censored parts of your selves in order to settle within the boundaries of the other. You have reined in the interests or passions that are part of your natural selves. Examples include: being playful or silly, being as smart as you are, finding the humor even in your stresses, and being a competent lover. These and more have all become tailored to fit the backgrounds and anticipations that you've accepted about your partner. This is how the ground soil of the BARK cycle gets tilled. You are both busy reducing each other. The fear that "being all you can be" may be offensive to the other is strong and you settle for the edited versions of yourself and "each other". The status quo is nailed in place until such fears are surpassed.

GOOD NEWS: A small part of being your full self is OK. You don't have to suddenly do the whole enchilada.

Just pick a new pattern small enough to be different but not too scary and try it out. You deserve to be surprised.

(Zinkler, J. 1977 *Creative Process in Gestalt Therapy*)

SERIOUSNESS:

Science has a proven record and relies on serious experimentation. However, the human adventure often requires leaps to be made by tinkering playfully with possibilities. Getting over rough spots together often calls for humor and wit as well as stern minded problem solving. Season any PEAK attempts with plenty of each. Beware of over-certainty. It deadens interactions and arouses defenses.

STUPIDITY:

Dull minds miss good chances. The differences between intelligence and ignorance are important! Since you've read this far already your intellect is not in question. Even the best of minds carry burdens of ignorance. What is unknown or undiscovered remains the challenge of scientific research.

There is also a difference between ignorance and lack of awareness. What you don't know is different from what you are not aware of. Awareness grows as you observe and notice the effects and patterns that occur within yourself and your partner. Awareness myopia shrinks one's strength and imagination. Possibilities get buried and hope is diminished. Education drifts away. PEAK into this by noticing what you have ignored and what you have avoided as well as what makes things work well for both of you.

Study what it is you want to learn; Learn what you study!

POLITENESS:

Politeness and courtesy are almost the same. In relationships there are differences between the two. Politeness often means ***Don't make waves*** or ***Keep your thoughts to yourself***. But waves need to be made when the relationships are ill. The choice is often to either be true to yourself or protect your partner.

Courtesy means to allow both of you to have access to the truth. Disasters are often followed by the lament: "Why didn't you tell me?"

Polite people avoid being pushy or aggressive. They hesitate to stand up and allow their truths to be heard.

Courteous people are respectfully assertive with the intention to exert influence for self and for others. Creative PEAKING involves courtesy.

Self-Limiting Beliefs

These are beliefs about yourself, your abilities, your worth, and what other people think of you. They are there as the result of all the Bark cycles you have accumulated. They represent your less favorable views of your personal history. Just like the (A)ANTICIPATION part of the BARK cycle, they are your faulty predictors of who you are becoming and how you will make choices and manage your life style. They also govern the degree by which you feel you deserve to belong effectively within your relationships.

In contrast to "being all you can be", these beliefs limit your potential and form many "can'ts", "won'ts", "shouldn'ts", and "only ifs". Being less than you are or less than you could be keeps you in the BARK cycle and gives you trouble when it's PEAK time to *Activate Resources*.

ABOUT BELIEVING BELIEFS

Since we have both freedom and liberty, is there really an imperative to have beliefs? One characteristic of people known to live their lives well is that they tend to have a reasonable toleration for uncertainty. (Maslow, A.H. (1962) *Toward a Psychology of Being)*. Compared to 'know-it-alls', authorities, tyrants, and 'true believers' – those who live well – claim no convenient path to enlightenment. They accept that getting near the truth is hard work and usually imperfect. They are decisive primarily in their patience and healthy skepticism. Truth propositions are tested with rigor before conclusions are permitted. Even then, such conclusions remain provisional. That is why respected statistical *truths* carry probability notations and error of measurement statements.

Having inherited the switchboards mentioned earlier, how do we come to know who we are and what to believe about ourselves?

From the first challenges of life, we learn that there are problems within us and around us. We have to decide what to do about them. Each decision made leads to a cluster of beliefs that form around who we are and how to cope with ourselves and with others. We soon learn that ignoring the glitches and grinches will work only temporarily and not too well anyhow. By trial and error solutions are located. The ones that work quickly turn into beliefs. These beliefs become guidelines for how to do battle within ourselves and with our world. Some of these beliefs become 'vows' and these 'vows' form strong and firm policies of identity and action.

Your early childhood beliefs and vows were not blessed with advantages of experience or maturity. They locked in place unchallenged and unedited. They operate to restrict you, your values, and your behaviors and prevent you from getting out of hand. They also help you plan for at least survival, if not victory.

If you fail to form enough of these vows and beliefs on your own, your peers, adults and cultures are ready and willing to fill in the blanks. The searches for truths are often preempted by your own constraints and by the accepted intrusions from other sources. Beliefs and vows, some of which may have become obsolete remain in charge of your life until revised. Such revision is the requirement when hope recedes and BARKING is squelching the juices out of faltering relationships.

Examples: "I am not good at taking tests"

                    "I will never fall in love again"

                    "It's too late to start over again"

                    "I'm not very lovable"

For these and others like them, useful questions would be" "How did I get this one?"; "Who did I get this one from?"; "What does believing this one do for me?" ; "What advantage(s) would I give up if this belief were no longer true for me??"; "Are there ways to enjoy those advantages without insulting myself???"; "Can I rewrite this one to make it much healthier for myself?"

TO CHECK THE VALIDITY OF A LIMITING BELIEF:

A. Wait until you are ready to privately step back and review relationship situations that have not gone well for you.

B. Replay the choices you made while responding to your partner.

C. Sort out the choices that were effective and keep those for later. Locate the ones that did not work well for you.

D. ASK: *What did I believe that led to my making those choices?*

E. Either write or type out the words of such belief or say them out loud in real words.

F. Find the words that have universal or absolute meaning and cancel out any flexible choice. (phrases like I will never...; I will always...; no way...; must...; can't... etc.)

G. *Determine the costs and advantages of such limits.* Decide if such beliefs work for You. Wait until you are ready to privately step back and review situations that have not gone well for you.

Replay the choices you made in responding to the other person(s).

Sort out the choices that were effective and keep those for later. Locate the ones that didn't work well.

Ask: "What did I believe about me that led to my making those choices"?

H. Either write or type out the words of such a belief or say them out loud or to yourself in real words.

Find the words in such a belief that have universal or absolute meaning and therefore cancel out any flexible choice. (phrases like: "I will never"; "I will always"; "no way"; etc)

Check to see if you really do believe this to be true for you, or if you have room for doubt.

Our world is beset with absolute passions of true believers Who have no rooms for doubt. Campaigns of death and destruction, based on faulty intelligence have called humanity into its wars with Ourselves.

No need for couple relations to be dispirited by absolutistic beliefs about either the limitations of ourselves or the potentials of each of us to the other.

Believe your limitations if you must - challenge each when you P.E.A.K.!

Revising an Obsolete Belief

Self-limiting beliefs do the limiting because there are gaps in the information. They also distort the information available and apply it to universal situations despite being based on one episode or cluster of events from your past. These beliefs remain in place because they have become habitual and unchallenged parts of your identity. They provide excuse for your failings and set expectations well within your comfort levels. They keep you where you have been. Revising them becomes relevant when it comes time for you to get off your duff and do a better job. (Andreas C.R. & Andreas (!989) Heart of the Mind).

Because it is a belief, you have to figure out what to believe about it. That involves getting a handle on how you sort for what is true and what is doubtful.

Make it easy: What do you see, hear, feel, and tell yourself when you know something is true? Ex: I know the door is locked because....!

When you doubt something, what do you see, hear, feel, or tell yourself?

Ex: The door may not be locked because.....!

Go back to the last Barking cycle you two had and practice which parts of it are true for you and which are not.

How do you know what's true? How do you know what is to doubt?

Once you have the standards for when you are in a state of truth, as well as the contrasting standards for when you are in a state of doubt.

Write here: Standards for **TRUTH** (believing): See? Hear? Feel? Say?

Standards for **DOUBTING** See? Hear? Feel? Say?

Next step: Either say aloud or write down one of your self-limiting beliefs. Use your typical language. Record it here:

PEAK! : Edit and rewrite by changing one word at a time to make the belief more respectful of who you really are. Write the edited belief here:

Check it for gaps, distortions, or generalizations.

Test, adjust, re-test as much as needed to get the new belief consistent with the health of your mind, body, and spirit before completing this process. See details of the TOTE (test-operate-test) procedures in later pages.

When you are ready, place the old limiting belief into your collection of obsolete antiques.

Enter the new belief into your collections of TRUTH and abilities for Getting Along With Yourself and Your Partner. Tinker with new beliefs whenever awkwardness appears.

PEAK POSTULATE: Facts about yourself are friendlier than fantasies about yourself.

They deserve careful maintenance.

The Sequential chart for doing the above steps is repeated on following page.

How to change a self-limiting Belief
(To be in meta position means to be located in your most capable, mature,
and analytical observation mode.)

Step one: Get yourself into

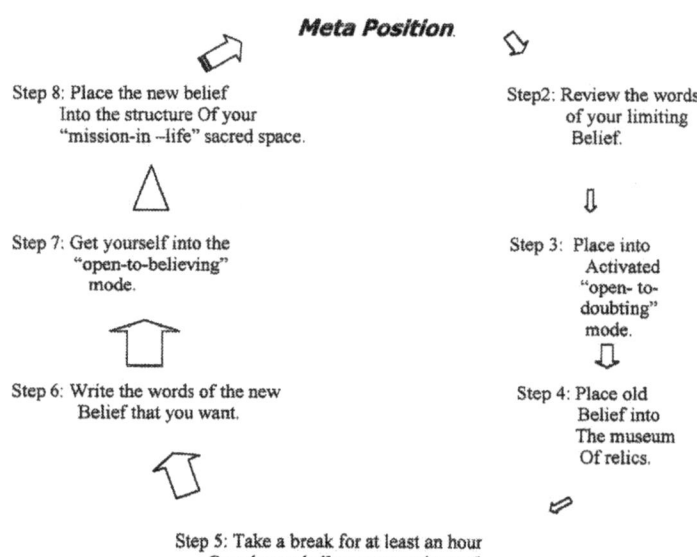

Meta Position.

Step 8: Place the new belief
Into the structure Of your
"mission-in –life" sacred space.

Step 7: Get yourself into the
"open-to-believing"
mode.

Step 6: Write the words of the new
Belief that you want.

Step2: Review the words
of your limiting
Belief.

Step 3: Place into
Activated
"open- to-
doubting"
mode.

Step 4: Place old
Belief into
The museum
Of relics.

Step 5: Take a break for at least an hour
Or a day and allow your caring and
capable self to sort through old limits
and the new potentials.

Note* Meta Position means to be located in your most capable, mature, analytical observation mode.

Next step: Either say aloud or write down one of your self-limiting beliefs. Use your typical language. Record it here:

PEAK! : Edit and rewrite by changing one word at a time to make the belief more respectful of who you really are. Write the edited belief here:

Check it for gaps, distortions, or generalizations.

Test, adjust, re-test as much as needed to get the new belief consistent with the health of your mind, body, and spirit before completing this process. See details of the TOTE (test-operate-test) procedures in later pages.

When you are ready, place the old limiting belief into your collection of obsolete antiques.

Enter the new belief into your collections of TRUTH and abilities for Getting Along

With Yourself and Your Partner. Tinker with new beliefs whenever awkwardness appears.

PEAK POSTULATE: Facts about yourself are friendlier than fantasies about yourself.

They deserve careful maintenance.

The Sequential chart for doing the above steps is shown on page 44.

Note* Meta Position means to be located in your most capable, mature, analytical observation mode.

<u>VOWS</u>

Vows are special forms of limiting beliefs. They tell what you must be and do as well as what you must not be or do. Your Vows have been made as you were passing through turning points in your life. Vows persist after the concerns under which they were formed become obsolete.

Public Vows are promises to others or to the world. Public vows taken under coercion will function largely at the convenience of the *Vower.*

(A prime flaw of political promises)

Private *Vows* are made in the interests of survival, love, and commitments to your morals , ethics, your *Life Mission,* and your relationships.

All vows require sacrifice. Your strong private vows define your adulthood. Upgrading a vow often is a shift from I will never….. to I will always.. Replace a restricitive vow with a generative one.

Editing a vow: Write down the words of the original vow in question right here:

Remember the "turning point" in your life under which you formed the vow. Decide how you were feeling when you decided on this vow.

With the help of what you now know that you didn't know and understand back at that time, rewrite that vow to make it effective in meeting current responsibilities in your life realities. Write the revision(s) Here:

Go back through time to your younger self at the turning pont and compare the two vows for healthiest results, both then and now. Check for any cost of change in the new vow.

Locate future situations when you want to use any revisions of your vow and plan to use them at such times and places.

YOUR TIMELINES

Streams of time, like your favorite river, flow from the beginnings of your life, your jobs, and your relationships up until your now. When you are in the flowing currents of that stream, you'll be "wet" all over and have limited choices about how to swim. You'll find yourself going with the flow and hoping the flow will carry you where you want to be. If it does, you can thank your lucky stars as well as divine providence. If it isn't, you can climb out and stand on shore long enough to see where you have been and look at what's up ahead.

Here are some features of how you operate when you are "in" the flow of time:

You tend to get caught up in the moment.
You are frequently late.
You avoid setting deadlines.
Your emotions are intense.
You are impulsive in making choices.

These are features of how you operate when you are on shore and watching the entire stream:

You can view what's happened and what's likely to happen.
You are usually on time.
You stay on task until the job is done.
You can formulate plans and outcomes.
You are careful in making choices.

It may be obvious that when it's time to have fun, make love, relax, go to a party, or enjoy the essences of being alive, you are best to be right in the stream of time.

When it's time to get the job done, manage you life style, be responsible, or get into your executive mode, it would be wise to be onshore getting the best available view of things. (James T. & Woodsmall. W :1988.; Andreas C. & Andreas S.: 1988)

It may be equally obvious that being stuck inside the stream or stuck onshore may be in violation of your knowledge that *persistence* is a virtue up intil the moment it becomes *stubbornness.*

Flexibility of choice about where and when to be – as time goes by – is a mark of being an adult. As time passes, couples often work out implicit deals which call for which one to be where during selected situations.

Couples are often confounded when one is on the shore and the other is in the stream at the wrong time or place. their structure may well crash and burn when both partners together are either "in" or "on shore" for stubborn reasons.

The ultimate splendor comes when a harmony is fashioned within your Couple space that will make use of the talents of each and the forces of your connections.

The following four R's will be useful in designing and working out such SPLENDOR and HARMONY :

RESPECT for each one's unique differences of perception and talent.

RESPONSIBILITY for intentions and choices for individual and couple interests.

RESPONSIVENESS to unplanned or unexpected challenges to each or to the couple.

RESOURCEFULNESS to activate new patterns when the old ones stop working.

None of us knows how far into the future each of our TIMELINES will extend, but we do know that they extend forward from the NOW. You can be *on shore* now with choices about how to design a compelling stream toward a future strong enough to guide you and your partner to destinations that fulfills both of your dreams. Stream forward with wisdom.

Chapter Five:

PEA"K"

KEEPING WHAT WORKS

(ONLY AS LONG AS IT WORKS)

This is both the hard part and the tender part. If the new pattern works for you, enjoy the gain! If it works for you but not your partner, keep it and tinker with it. If it works for both of you, appreciate it.

New things that work are the beginnings of habits. Good habits are healthy until they become "robot-like". They are the first resort when troubles arise. When you do what has always worked and it either does not fit the situation or has become obsolete to your partner, you have re-entered a BARK cycle and it is time to PEAK anew.

Example: When Eugene and Thelma were first getting serious with one another, they had a lover's spat. Eugene was lost about what to do. One of his buddies advised him to send her a single red rose with a well-selected card. It worked! All was forgiven and true love was resumed. For years well into their marriage, it worked until Thelma exploded in anger:

Thelma: *Don't ever send me another rose for the rest of your life! You can't get off that easy! It's been a* *phony way for you to get out of serious trouble and I've had it with your surface pretending that things are OK when there is a lot wrong he*re!

Eugene: It was always OK with you what's wrong now?

Thelma*: This is Stupid! You have no idea what is going on because you never ask. Your family always covered up their troubles and a (.....)ing rose won't cover ours.*

Eugene: Well what do you want me to do now?
Thelma: **Grow up!**

If Eugene knows about the PEAK model, it would be good for him to enter it at this point. Even if he doesn't know about it, he should get rid of the rose thing, and invent some other way to act when things are crash landing between he and Thelma. The same is true for Thelma; PEAK patterns are useful regardless of gender or role between people who care about one another.

The tender part involves diversity and artistry. Investors hear much about "diversification" and not "putting all their eggs on one basket". The PEAK potential is loaded with options available to prevent robot-like habit patterns from mindless repetition on cue.

Artistry can be both the tender part and the fun part. Maybe artistry is one of the overlooked secrets to relationship health. You are given abilities to make being together more than obligation, duty, ritual, or toleration. Humor and conversation are constant opportunities to enrich your processes of being together. Being artful is not automatic. You must move beyond the ground zero of your own boredom and raise energy to meet the interests of the other's presence

We tend to think of artists as an especially talented group apart from most of us. They provide music, entertainment, color and special crafts that form our cultures and enrich our lives. They can't do it all for us. We must tend to our own tapestries.

While keeping what is working, keep your resources active. When you are about to repeat a pattern that is working, find ways to add freshness or uniqueness to it. Activate your resources!

Recovering and Activating Resourceful States

Times come along when you need your very best self to be able to do the right thing(s). The chart below is a map for organizing the best moments of your personal history. It is also a map for creating patterns for future use in demanding situations.

Remember a time when you surprised yourself by doing something you had thought to be impossible. Write your answers in each section below:

EXTERNAL	INTERNAL
What were you looking at when you did it?	What are you seeing in your "mind's eye" as you remember doing it?
What did you hear at the moment of success?	What do you say to yourself as you triumph?
What were you touching/ doing/feeling as you were succeeding?	Imagine stepping inside those moments and describe the emotions:
What was the taste/smell of success as it was happening?	Write here a smell and a taste that are typical when you see-hear-feel success.

You may find it useful to repeat this chart for a selection of different successes important to you.

Review the chart(s) and select parts of each that are easiest to access and allow them to link you to resources appropriate for the challenge at hand. Remind yourself of situations where you may ignore or forget that you can do this and attach a good **SIGNAL TO MOVE YOUR BEST SELF INTO ACTION!**

<u>Caring Deeds</u>

Caring deeds are little things that each of you can do for one another. These are things that make life kinder and softer for each of you, and for "Getting along together".

There are three reasons why you two often don't get what you want:
1. You don't know what it is.
2. You haven't asked for it.
3. When & where are not specific.

Here is a chart for organizing and improving times and places for offering "Caring Deeds". Make copies for each of you. Start with just one per person per week and see how it goes. Write into the "want" spaces what is wanted. Put check marks for when you did and for when you got. If it works, experiment with additional deeds, times, or places.

You did	I want:	I got
I did	You want:	You got
We did	We want:	We Got

Sometimes you think you've done what your partner wanted but it didn't meet the other person's criteria. (There may be no check mark under "got".) Rework what is wanted and how to improve the doing of it!

Chapter Six:

ADVANCED PEAKS

SKILLS TO MASTER
Giving
Taking
Seeking
Feedback

GIVING OF SELF SKILLS

Whether wealthy or destitute, SELF is what we have to give to the people who are significant in our lives. Friends and lovers are fond of saying things like " I will be there for you". More than just saying such things, doing them with skill comes next in the PEAK life style. Skillful entry into the "here and now" is essential in breaking the BARK cycle.

PHYSICAL,MENTAL, ATTITUDE, PRESENCES

The important thing is to actually be in the location where the giving is to be done. Your physical presence is the first component of self –giving. You permit others to look upon you, to hear your voice, to know that you are here and not in some other place. You give eye-contact;

touches; appropriate locations, postures, and gestures; and real attention.

Mental and attitude dimensions are both potent elements of your presence, since it is possible to be physically in one location but thinking and/or feeling in other locations simultaneously. You give to the other person(s) your awareness of their presence and your investment in the processes of both of you.

The time dimension is also critical to skillful self-giving. It is possible to be focused on the past or the future despite what is currently happening right now. Thus self-giving involves your fullness of living right here and right now. You give to the other person(s) and yourself an awareness of mutual contact in the moment of concern.

Staying in the "here and now" is important only when the matter is of obvious importance to either you, the other person, or to both of you. Getting to the "here and now" is important when something needs to be changed or improved between you and the people you care about. Staying in the "there and then" will often lead to reviews of history, predictions of the future, or argument, avoidance, denial, and placing blame. Under 'there and then' conditions, rapport is lost and there is small hope of positive change.

Remember that you can make choices only about what you say or do. The choices of how all other persons respond are what you do not have control over. The only question for you is: *Can I do or say something that will improve chances that the other(s) will respond in ways that improve things for any of us?* If you can get into the NOW, chances will improve. The risk is that you may become more vulnerable, since you are being truthful rather than hiding behind the past or the future, or some other kind of smoke screen. Indirect communications tend to yield indirect or irrelevant responses and hopes for improvement may fade easily.

Giving of yourself means letting the other(s) know what is happening within you, and is a genuine gift even though what's in the gift may include unpleasant parts. At least with such knowledge there is a chance for positive change for all involved. The TRUST factor is huge here. Who do you choose to trust with your inside truths - Yourself or the other(s)?

MORE GIVING OF SELF SKILLS:

Self-disclosure means letting your "in-here" things pass into the "out there" world. You describe what is going on within you. Doing this effectively is a real skill. Conventional conversation emphasizes sharing of only low or no risk information about your self. The skill begins with awareness. You must know what is true for you in order to share it. Getting in touch with inside events requires effort. We are taught to censor or ignore many of these reactions in our growing up processes.

SELF-ASSERTION means making realities out of your possibilities. Use your strengths rather than withhold them. Owning your weaknesses makes them into guideposts rather than hidden traps. Acting on your talents rather than denying them enriches your living and stimulates the other lives you touch. Take responsibility for your own choices rather than depend upon outside forces to direct what happens to you. Choose how to regard your situations and how you choose what to do about them.

SELF-EXPRESSION involves artistry. Your words can be enhanced by timing, tone changes, volume, pauses, word selection, and attitude. Your visual messages can be amplified by eye contact, smiles, postures, and gestures. When these elements are consistent with what is inside, your messages are clear. When they are inconsistent, phoniness is the result. PEAK by practicing your artistry so that you can match your expressions with your experiences. This skill is often labeled *genuineness* or *congruence*.

TAKING (listening)

When one has something to give and there are no takers, this is not good! Taking, in itself, is often regarded as a no-no, easily related to selfishness or even stealing. So let's change "taking" to "accepting". Would that work better? To accept well usually means you have to have been paying attention or you'd be getting stuff you wouldn't know you are getting. So let's try even a different word: "attending". Simplest form of this is LISTENING. So now we'd have some one GIVING and someone TAKING and a conversation could begin with each person alternating the giving with the taking. Now this is a simple formula for communicating. Problem is when it's time for us to "take" we often get busy deciding what to give back - and we do this while the other person is still talking. So what we give back is often disconnected from what the other person just gave. This is the end of conversation and the beginning of competition. Have you ever seen it?: Everyone giving and no one taking. When this happens, the stage is set for arguments, winning/losing and being lonely! **PEAK POSTULATE:** "Do not start talking until after the other person has stopped!"

Skillful "taking" means that you avoid planning what you are going to say while the other person is still talking. Keep your intake channels open to receive/accept

/take what your partner is giving you. Even if you don't agree with it or are offended by it, you can now confirm that you did hear it. (Rogers, Carl, 1974.*On Becoming a person)*

Fine points of TAKING skills

ENABLING – OBSERVING – APPRECIATING

Enabling is a word that means "to make it possible" to talk further by minimizing your competition with your partner. You can reduce defensiveness by accepting what is said rather than finding flaws in it or trying to top the other story. Try to reduce such responses like "yes, but"; "that may be true, but.."; "on the other hand"; or "did you ever consider that…." Instead, use simple expressions such as: "mmhhhmm", "I see", "Oh", "interesting", or "never thought of it that way" ***PEAK POSTULATE***: It is not necessary to correct all of your partner's errors in thinking immediately!

Observing means to listen with the third ear. You take in greater amounts of meaning by observing posture, movement, eye expressions, voice tone, and breathing. Hear the words, the intention behind the words, and see the acts of physical communication. **PEAK POSTULATE:**

Over 90 % of meanings exchanged in relationships are due to non-verbal messages.

Appreciating means that when the other person produces a positive message you quickly provide a positive response to it. Smiling, leaning forward, making eye contact, saying words like "good"; "I like that"; or "thank you"; are simple examples. These are not hard to do and the may protect each of you from crash landings in "Barkhood". ***PEAK POSTULATE***: Positive reinforcement really does work!

SEEKING (Asking)

If you choose to risk vulnerability by telling the truth within you, it would help to find out some truth about what's inside the other(s). Seeking this information takes two forms: asking closed questions or asking open questions. A closed question is one that can easily be answered with a brief or one word response. An open question is one that requires elaboration and is difficult to answer with one or two words.

Lawyers, seeking to establish facts often ask closed questions designed for "yes" or "no" answers and establish small chunks of truth. Closed questions often begin with the letter "D": "Did you see the crime"?; "Didn't you hear the shot"?; "Doesn't it seem true?; etc. "W" questions also are easy to answer briefly: Why did you? When were you there? What happened next? *Why* questions often lead to excuses or justification stories.

Open questions are often not questions, but rather instructions that begin with the letter "T": "Tell me about what you are thinking"; "Talk about what is real for you"; "Try to help me understand what's going on". If you put a "please" at the beginning of such instruction or request, it probably helps. Courtesy in the context of turmoil may be the soul of diplomacy, if not effectiveness. Actually, there may be times when a shift from aggression to courtesy may get the job done and not require either kind of SEEKING.

Seeking is part of the foundation for all negotiation efforts. Find out what is bugging the other party or what is needed or wanted in order to find out if you can make a better deal for all involved. If you have done decent jobs of GIVING and TAKING and then have used good SEEKING skills, you will enjoy improved chances to share vulnerabilities and forge new ways which require less competition or defensiveness.

To be good with these simple "SEEKING" abilities, most of us have had to overcome long established habits of language, relationship, and communication style. This takes listening to the "d's" and "w's" that creep mindlessly into the ways you use to seek information , and practicing to shift from closedness to openness unless you are "Lawyering".

Remember the "PEAK" model: pick and practice new and different behaviors to get improved results. Give the other(s) a break! Seeking does not mean "pinning the other one(s) down". It means finding out things that may work for all involved, including yourself.

FEEDBACK

Feedback means to let other(s) know how they are effecting you. It is the best way you have to clear static out of the way when things are not going well between you and the people you care about. If you do it well and properly time it, the chances of miscommunication can be reduced. Everyone has the chance to be on the same wave-length. In a way, skillful feedback is a form of advanced self-giving. It gives the others, as well as you a fresh start when things have gone awry.

There are two types of feedback : CONSTRUCTIVE & CONSTRICTIVE. CONSTRUCTIVE feed back is that which urges your partner toward positive outcomes.

Constrictive feedback is that which urges your partner to avoid negative outcomes.

Do give information about things the other person(s) can change. (Not about being too short, or having been born in the wrong family, etc)

Do identify words or actions that harm or effect your relationship.

Consider These Schemes:

CONSTRUCTIVE FEEDBACK IS POSITIVE	CONSTRICTIVE feedback is negative:
(attends what is correct or to shared difficulties)	(attends to flaws of others)
(reinforces desired behaviors)	(attempts to stop mistakes)
(is based on what you can see or hear)	Judges or Criticizes
Expletive: AHAH!	Expletive: OOPS!
Philosophy: "isism"	Philosophy:"shouldism"
Improvement - Expansion – Aliveness	Obedience/Worry/ Shrinkage/Defeat

General postulate; Couples who get along well together tend to make more positive feedback choices than negative ones.

Fine Points of Feedback Skills

1. Make descriptions rather than judgements.

Being evaluated or judged is one of the primary barriers to fluent communication. It raises hell with trust. We tend to personalize remarks made about our actions. Example: You say "that was a dumb mistake". Your partner then, is just a short way from receiving that as "I am both dumb and a mistake". So if you are going to evaluate, be sure to separate the evaluating of things, actions, or jobs from evaluating the person.

Evaluating or judging means to assign value or worth – good, bad, right, wrong, - and tends to become moralistic. When all the laws and ethics are lined up and imposed upon your partner, rapport is likely to suffer serious damages.

2. Describing means to express immediate sensory perceptions (what you actually see, hear, touch, feel smell or taste). Skillful descriptions frequently begin with the pronoun "I "or the word "IT". You then inform your partner about what you have witnessed and how it is effecting you. When feedback is done well, the other person will have improved chances to make change in a free way because there is less defensiveness generated.

3. Skilled feedback is focused upon describing the actions of your partner and how those actions or thoughts have effected you, **not** controlling the other person. Give feedback about things your partner can change, but not about being too short or tall or having been born in the wrong family! Describe to your partner, the things you appreciate. Also describe words or actions that have harmful effects on you in the relationship.

2. Otherness, Selfishness, and Selfness

We have traditionally been an "other" oriented culture. We've been taught to appear to be unselfish and to spend our efforts trying to figure out what it is that other people need or want. We can then place them in our debt by providing these things for them. This is one reason why it is difficult to get your partner to tell you what is wanted.

Most of us are wary about the obligatory trade. It's hard for both of us to dismiss our self interests.

"Don't be selfish" is one of our first powerful instructions as children. It takes on the character of Original Sin and is regarded as being unkind or inconsiderate. Being selfish becomes a serious "NO - NO" and appropriately so. For a selfish person, everyone else is lucky to make it to second place. Things are managed in a win/lose style which inevitably evolves into lose/lose reuslts.

Since each of us does have a self that requires healthful attention to remain alive, we must take care of ourselves. The Golden Rule, which urges that we give of ourselves , would have little meaning if there were no self from which to give. Many of our heroes are complimented by being called *selfless* because they have made sacrifices; some make the ultimate sacrifice. But selfless people often disappear and this is especially true in the social systems called relationships. Two selfless people don't get along together - they get along apart. This is even worse than the BARK cycle.

Selfness then becomes necessary to Get Along Together. Your relationship is formed between two selves that agree that living life is enriched when you have access to each other's selves. As your time together has grown, the inevitable differences in these two selves have become more clearly defined. Shared difficulties begin to cloud the ideals of being together well. Each of you does things or is ways that violate the preferences of the other. Sooner or later we irritate each other and frequently we don't know what we've done or how we've been that has led to these results. This is when skilled feedback becomes essential to get things back on tilt. **PEAK POSTULATE:** Effective feedback to your partner comes from the truths within your real self and how things are for you within the relationship.

Sample self-descriptive feedback statements:

Thelma: "I am sad about what is happening between us".

Eugene: "I want you to stop interrupting".

Thelma: "I need you to be fair".

Eugene: "OK, let's start this over – at the beginning.

Notice that each of the above samples has a period at the end, not a ? or a ! Each is a statement. The last is a request or suggestion. AM, NEED, WANT are key words of awareness in describing yourself. Selfness respects such awareness and the exchange between partners rests upon intentional feedback.

3. TOLERATE AMBIGUITY RATHER THAN DEMAND ABSOLUTES

A very natural human tendency is to bring closure (assign truth) to any issue as quickly as possible rather than experience ambiguity (not knowing the truth when all the requirements for knowing it are not yet assembled). Neat packages are easier to organize, but often turn out to be fraudulent.

"Knowing it all" or pretending to know it frequently places barriers between people. The use of absolutistic words like "always, never, ought, should, shouldn't, and can't" often interfere with good communication. They tend to increase argumentation or defensiveness. Your willingness to keep an issue open or to help your partner to do so may lead to deeper qualities of interaction. You can make this possible by intentional reduction of your use of absolutistic words and increasing provisional words like "sometimes, possibly, maybe, when, often, consider", etc.

4. REQUEST RATHER THAN DEMAND

While many of us like strong leadership, the experience of being ordered can be unpleasant and frequently evokes sabotage within relationships. When providing feedback, you wish to effect change by the other person in order to enhance the relationship.

Demanding often results in immediate outward change, but the accompanying inward changes can be very destructive. Thus it is important to use skillful requests. A skillful request usually has two parts:

A: Do your Selfness description.
B: Make a request for a change.

Sample:

Eugene: I am sad about how we got so angry, please help me understand.

Thelma: I don't want to talk about it.

Eugene: I am even sadder now, let's take a break, and talk later before dinner. * note: it is helpful to propose a specific time or location rather than just leaving at "later".

Thelma: We'll see.

Eugene: That's hopeful to me, so let's see together.

PEAK POSTULATE: Honor your selfness, respect your partner, tend to your shared relationship, describe your truth, request a change.

Robert E. Saltmarsh

Chapter Seven:

PLATFORMS FOR NEGOTIATING

1A. Negotiating with your self
100. The BARK check list
101. You- me- us- proposal
102. Principled negotiations
103. Reconcilable differences
104. Details about Rapport

<u>Negotiating with your self</u>

Before entering any negotiating, it will be useful to know about your part in the issues at hand. Here is an outline and work sheet that will help sort and clarify the choices you have been making.

1. Confront what you said and did.

   I said: ....

   I did: ....

2. Confront the thoughts and feelings the led to #1 above.

   I was thinking:..
   I was feeling:..

3. Label the above patterns:

What I wanted to happen was:.............................

My behaviors were:..

4. Clarify the functions of the above patterns.

I reacted that way in order to get or avoid:...............

....

5. Consider the consequences.

What then happened was:......................................

6. PEAK – allow alternatives.

So my preferred outcome(s) would be:......................

....

7. Review personal history successes.

In similar situations I have tried:...........................

....

8. Locate the best results.

I like what happened when:...................................

9. Choose.

So, at least for now I am going to:...........................

Test yourself:

Before you respond to your partner, Check: Is it true? Is it kind? Is it necessary?

Are your promises real and do you keep them faithfully?

Do you notice the good things and give credit for them?

Can you dismiss gossip and negativity?

Can you believe your partner does the best that's possible with the information available?

Can you disagree without being disagreeable?

Can you have a discussion not an argument?

Can you stop, turn around, take three breaths, and count to ten before inflicting hurt on your partner?

Can you allow your virtues to speak for themselves?

Of all human things, virtue itself is its own reward. (Marcus Aurelius)

Is your sense of humor active and available?

Console more than be consoled? Understand as much as be understood? Love as much as be loved?

Platforms for Negotiating

When you two get stuck in "Barking" with each other, or when your "Peaks" are not working well, it is time to negotiate.   Here are some "platform" models that will help you get stated:

Platform 100:   "The BARK check list"

Check each one that is true:

Background: I use yours against   You use mine
                  you__.   against me__

Anticipations: I use mine against   You use yours
                  you__.   against me__

Rudeness: I am rude to   You are rude to
                  you__.   me__.

Knicks: I am saving all of   You are saving all
                  mine__.   of yours__.

This platform is the simplest place to begin, but it is both crude and accusative so be careful. Use it more for your self than your partner to locate changes you can make. If you can use it together, it may show what changes would help for both of you.

Negotiation wisdom: Practice privately before using the platform you select. Use the easiest option first. If it doesn't work, advance to the next level. Remember "baseball" (three strikes before you're out).

When/where to negotiate? The first answer is now and here! The better answer is when we've cooled down and at an agreed upon time and place. The problem is that when you're both feeling better, neither wants to drag up the bad stuff. Think of negotiating as a joint search for better stuff, rather than plunging back into the toxins. Set up a separate time and a comfortable place. Successful negotiating results in gains for all and less pain for each.

Platform 101: "You – Me – Us – Proposal"

This platform is basic, simple, and fair. You try to tell the truth about your partner, about yourself, and about your "us". Then you propose what could be done to improve things for You, Me, and Us.

You: To do this part, you will have to make your best guess about what is going on within you partner and put in words that fit well for her/him – an expression of empathy.

"Empathy" means to understand what it's like for the other person and to say it well enough that he/she feels understood.

Me: Here is where you tell the truth about what is happening within you. These are the basic "Self-Giving-Self-Disclosure" skills described in earlier pages. It is important to do this as you relate to the current situation between the two of you. Do not attempt to leak over into "global" concerns. Get out your truth about this one, knowing that there is no one more expert on you than you.

Us: Describe your version of "US" and ask for your partner's version. Talk about the difference(s) between "how things are" and "how you want them to be". Agree on at least one of those differences that you both have the power to change.

PROPOSAL: Say out loud what you think will reduce the differences and make things better. Listen to what your partner says and ask for their proposal. Discuss the ways each of you can get more of what you want from one another and form a plan that includes both time and place for change.

Platform 102: "Principled Negotiations"

(Fisher, R. and Ury, W.: Getting to Yes , 1981)

Principle 1.   Separate the persons from the problems, and behaviors from intentions. We easily distinguish between the presidency and the person who is the president, and we know that a person who made a mistake is not a "mistake". Negotiating takes place between two people; not between two problems or two behaviors. It's purpose is to agree upon new choices which benefit both persons.

Principle 2.   Focus on underlying concerns (hopes, merits, and intentions) not positions of opposition. Negotiations are not arguments!

Principle 3.   Base efforts on objective standards and fair procedures:
A: What things are like when the two of you have been at your best.
B: What each of you will see, hear, feel, think when change is complete.

C: Prevailing standards for couples who get along well together.

Principle 4: Know your **best alternative to a n**egotiated **a**greement. (BATNA) This is your survival principle! Establish it well and keep it up to date with revisions as your wisdom and spirit expand. It is what you will keep valuable for yourself even if present negotiation fails.

Your BATNA includes at least: Knowledge that your self respect is intact; your interests have been presented; enhanced awareness of strengths and weaknesses, and revised strategies for next negotiations

(Fisher, R. and Ury, W.: *Getting to Yes* , 1981); Fisher.R. & Brown,S. 1998. *Getting* Together. Building Relationships As We Negotiate)

Things to say – Ways to talk:

Make a "self description". Describe your current feeling (s). Describe your intention(s). Describe your hope(s).

"I appreciate the chance to talk it over."

"Let's agree to be fair."

"Please correct me if what I say is not true for you."

"Let me see if I understand what you just said."

"Here is my suggestion "–"- Let me hear yours".

When it's tough to agree:

Switch roles for a short, specified time (ie 5 minutes). Then review impressions.

Write down points of agreement so far. Then allow each person to alternate one amendment at a time that advances the interests of each and the interests of "GETTING ALONG TOGETHER".

Brainstorm! Together, list as many ideas and possibilities for resolving differences.

List and sort all of them into priorities for feasibility and testing as you resume negotiating.

Agree to take a break, consult individually with trusted, unbiased third parties and resume negotiation at a specified time and place. A counselor may help. Make notes to yourself about your emotions, what you understand, how to use the skills from this book or from other sources.

A WISE AGREEMENT will be one that is better than your BATNA, and binds you both to realistic commitments.

When all of the above is intact, it is time for each of you to make suggestions that each of you can test for comfortable fit. Early suggestions may be editied until satisfactory to all involved. Before acceptance as a part of the eventual proposal , each should answer these questions:

Is it a Yes for you, me, and us?

Do each of you have control over getting it done at reasonable cost?

Will doing it damage any of the valuable parts of the total Togetherness?

Can you test it long enough and well enough to see if it works for all concerned?

When all four are fluent you will have completed this negotiation, and a new day is at hand. You will now be veterans at such negotiations. New life beckons you to your getting along together well.

Choice Boxes for Couples Final

		Your *Behavior*	
		Cooperate	Defect
		I win (CC)	I lose big (CD)
	Cooperate	You win.	You win big.
My *Behavior*			
		(DC)	(DD)
	Defect	I win big.	I lose
		You lose big.	You lose.

(Fisher, Roger and Brown Scott. 1988,Getting together-Building Relationships as We negotiate)

		You try to understand	*You do not try* to understand
I understand		We both understand each other.	I understand you, you do not understand me.
I do not try to understand you.		I don't understand you, but you understrand me well.	N e i t h e r understands, we continue to do poorly together

PEAK Pattern:Locate which box you are in and use any of the platforms for negotiation to move to a better box.

Platform 103: The "Reconcilable Differences" Platform

This platform calls for RISK knowledge. There are two things to know: Risk assessment and Risk management. Assessment means to know what the odds for success/ failure are likely to be. Also you must be truthful about whether the advantages of your relationship are at least equal or outweigh the alternative(s). When they do, you have "reconcilable differences", and it will be worth it to negotiate skillfully. Use any of the above platforms or combinations of them that match your comfort level. The key is to agree to reconcile the good stuff between you two, and to learn to tolerate or re-interpret the differences. That is how differences become "Reconcilable"!

Management means to select behaviors that support your goals and do them well enough to improve things for both of you. There are two types of errors you can make in managing RISK. Error #1: Doing something that turns out to be the wrong thing to do.

*Grievous errors: If you have reached the point where you have decided that you are never going to get what you want and are considering infidelity, the dangers are such that they may be irreparable. Go to you highest principles and values. The risks to all are perilous and the pains are severe. Error #2: Missing the chance to do the right thing.

To reduce error #1 Gather and validate as much relevant information as possible as you negotiate.

To reduce Error #2 Be alert and ready to PEAK and test "What if" or "As if" opportunities as you negotiate.

Be certain that any new agreement will make things better than before for both of you and that values sacred to each of you are preserved or altered only in acceptable ways

PEAK Postulate: The boundary between risk and folly is delicate. Be careful about what you want – you may get it.

Negotiating with Rapport works better than negotiating without Rapport.

Rapport means that honor, dignity, respect, and caring are obvious and available to each of you as you negotiate. Even when you disagree, these values must be intact. If Rapport is lost, the negotiators should agree to take a break and re-establish rapport as the first objective when you resume.

Details about rapport skills are described on the next three pages.

Abbreviations-Codes-Mindreadings

More than words are involved in the rapport structures of either Barking or Peaking. When you two were forming your early relationship, you were careful with every word you used. As time has passed, complete sentences are no longer required. Complex meanings can pass between you with just a glance, how you enter the room, skin color, the tone of a murmur or grunt, Etc. These are the codes or calibrations of your life together. Like the calibrated needles on the car speedometer or fuel gage which provide messages for decision-making. The calibrated less-than-verbal messages exchanged between you two are like a weather report. Such weather rapport informs each of you if there is a storm brewing or if the weather is fair.

Most of us do not have voluntary control over natural physiological responses. Yet Monks, actors, athletes, and biofeedback researchers have shown that we all can improve our influences over such reactions with awareness and practice. You are not stuck with having just to say the right thing at the right time (or vice versa).

One of the simplest rapport building decisions is for you to match the tempo and depth of your partner's breathing rate. Another is to take any calibrated (shortened or compact) message and fill it in with real words. Still another is to match the other's calibration before you try to change it. You don't have to be angry when the other person is angry, but you can match at least one of the calibrations before attempting any other influence.

Calibrations become habits for each of you. As such, unintended messages can corrupt your system: *An innocuous grunt from Eugene's sore joint and Thelma thinks he's about to buy a new car! Thelma lets the wind slam the door and Eugene thinks he's in deep doo* doo!

Details about Rapport

When you two have rapport, it feels good for each of you. When you don't have it, you've slipped back into the Bark Mode with each other, or become careless about your better ways of "Getting Along". While it's best if both of you work on regaining rapport, here are ways to start the process on your own:

Detail 1: Stop, Look, and Listen! Stop what you have been doing, look at your partner and listen to their messages. Then say back what you have heard with unbiased voice and tone. Sarcasm, cynicism, or criticism will not work well here. Silence is a message in itself. When in doubt, match the silence while looking and listening.

Detail 2: Match! Do at least one thing that your partner is doing. Match posture, position and movement. (Voice tempo, volume, or tone - along with gestures and word selection** are among things that can be matched).

**Word selection: At any moment your partner's messages will favor one of 3 sense catagories- Seeing; Hearing; Feeling. When you select words that match your partner's sense category, rapport will improve. See chart that follows.

Chart:Sense word lists

SEEING WORDS	HEARING WORDS	FEELINGS WORDS
picture	sound	touch
clear	say	handle
focus	hear	throw
see	ring	shock
flash	tune	stir
bright	static	hurt
cloudy	voice	pain
glimpse	loud	feel
color	tone	move
graphic	ask	hit
clarify	tell	rub
look	click	gentle
view	muffle	soothe
show	scream	relax
appear	alarm	fit

"Getting along together" is a bit easier when each person can learn to speak the language of the other. People who have easy rapport are automatically in sync with one another. Lost rapport will rebuild as intentional efforts restore rhythm and messages of one to the other.

Detail 3: Pace! Go at the same speed and rhythm of your partner.

Detail 4: Lead! Once you are doing all of the above, slightly alter one of them that is comfortable for you. Continue until your partner makes a similar change. Then you will know that the rapport between you is improving.

Detail 5: TOTE! Test – Operate – Test – Exit. This is the spirit guide for the PEAK MODEL!

TEST ONE: Are you satisfied with what is happening? Yes – Keep doing what you've been doing. No – Do something different.

OPERATE ONE: Select something different and the time and place to try it out. Try it out! Timing is important. Doing the right thing in the wrong context seldom works.

TEST TWO: Does it work well? For you? For your partner? For your relationship? Yes – Exit! When you get what you want, enjoy it! Don't mess with it until it doesn't work any more. No – Operate.

OPERATE TWO +: Do something different to make it better for you. Do something different to make it better for your partner. Do something different to make it better for both of you.

TEST THREE+: Remember the "baseball" model - three strikes before you are out on any of the above! The TOTE model recycles well and does not become obsolete. Whatever is stupid or ill formed will be deleted quickly with each testing. What is healthy and enhancing will be discovered sooner or later. Rapport will grow with each operation and each test.

Columbus used the TOTE model to discover the New World. When you think of it, TOTE is the skeleton of all science and discovery!

RAPPORT REVIEW:

1. STOP. LOOK. LISTEN!
2. MATCH!
3. PACE!
4. LEAD!
5. TOTE!

Flash points, anguish, despair.

These are the conditions under which we start wars, commit violence, and make uncorrectable mistakes. The crimes of passion explode when locked into the entanglements of these emotional extremes. The moment your teeth clench, your fist tightens, you urge to lash out, you are loosing your choice abilities. Get out of there now!! It may be too late to salvage what you once had. Any victory you achieve will cost so much that it will fade quickly. But it is never too late to exit the red zone if you recognize these conditions are building and your options are dwindling. Move away while you can! Get some distance in space first and time second. Especially in closed spaces like cars or small rooms, move away and keep your hands to yourself.

Do not lock into daring glares. Look away before looking back. Being the Alpha wolf is for animals. Count three deeper breaths. Do not insist on having the last word. Say mature things to yourself before you say any thing out loud. Remember that it is better to be safe than right, better to act with intention than to act with impulse, and better to heal than to be right. "It is better to be happy than to be right." (McGraw,P.C, Ph.D.,*Relationship Rescue 2000).* Keep your distance till the emotional intensity recedes out of the danger zone. Choose and define outcomes that are appropriate for you and select strategies to move toward them. Make sure the strategies are definable in actions you can control and preserve the life styles that work for you, and that you can test them. ***PEAK POSTULATE***: Use any part of what you read or learned in this book or from other sources, to get the healing processes active and underway for yourself and, if possible, for the other person.

Robert E. Saltmarsh

Chapter Eight:
DESIGNING A COMPELLING FUTURE

This is a future that is powerful and attractive enough to have a kind of magnetism that pulls you and your relationship toward it.   Futures are yours to design and engineer within the boundaries of not only your current life space, but also the space that evolves as you advance into your time line of the future. To keep it simple, start with one goal. You can build other features around it once you have it in place and know the drill: (Cameron-Bandler, Leslie 1985 *The Emprint Method & Know How. San rapheal, CA: Future Pace Inc.)*

Specify a time in your future when you will achieve a goal that will support you at your best. Mark it on an open calendar or on a drawn timeline of your future.

Check to make sure the goal is positively stated (what evidence ***will be there*** as opposed to what ***will not be*** there); Depends only on what actions you can control to achieve it; Preserves all other valuable parts of your life; and it is Testable for feasibility and desirable results.

Make a life-size image of yourself having achieved this goal at the identified time. Include details of what you will look like, your posture, breathing, movement, and body/mind/spirit congruence.

When all details fit together well, mentally step inside the image or put it on like a set of long underwear. Stay in there long enough to check it out and see if it would be OK for you. Then step back out of the image so you can take a look at all the actions that must take place between now and the completion of your goal.

Examine what you must do to complete each action that will lead to your desired future.

Place markers on your calendar or timeline to show when, where, and how each action must take place as you advance to completion of your goal. Label each action.

Convert each marker into signals of what you will see, hear, think, feel, and do when out there in the future flow of time; SIGNALS that will let you know that "NOW is the time to do the ACTION . Decide whether it would be best to "be in the flow" or "on the shore" as the signals for each action arrive.

Example: When it's 4th down and two, is it better to be "in the flow" or "on shore" when deciding whether to punt - or go for it?

Here is another set of clues:

From your own "BARK" patterns as well as other events in you personal history, you have accumulated a file of choices that turned out to be wrong! While it may be more comfortable to minmize, ignore, or forget them, they are clear evidence of what went wrong. They help define the famous "Roads Not Taken" as you've come this far in you life travels. These moments of past decision are now markers to help define what you Do want as well as what you Don't want. As it is popular to hear "what part of failure do you not understand?"—It may be equally useful to know all parts that have led to failures, and PEAK into better choices in your life styles for the future.

It is helpful to know the differences between solving problems and gaining outcomes.

Early science took form by solving problems. A problem had to be located before the science could proceed. Discovery and invention followed shortly and then science advanced from problem solving and was freed to locate outcomes and design ways to achieve them. In intimate relationships, It is fair to assume a ready supply of problems. Your choices for the future are whether to invest energies in the problem frame or move to the invitations of the outcome frame:

When you are in the problem frame:	When you are in the outcome frame:
1. Oops! Something is wrong.	A. Hmmmmm? What would be right?
2. Why is it wrong?	B. How could it change?
3. Because : Someone is to blame... It has never worked... Of stubborn limitations...	C. Experiment: PEAK!
4. Still Failing But knowing why!	D. Finding what would work...Making progress!

PEAK Points:

ACTIVATE YOUR RESOURCES: Review Chapter four.

ZOMBIE STYLE	RESOURCEFUL STYLE
I don't know.	I'll find out.
I can't help it.	I make a difference.
I can't.	I'll find a way.
Who cares?	I care.
So what?	Things matter.

Robert E. Saltmarsh

Chapter Nine:

Life Style:

Eight Ideas for Building and Enjoying Yours

The following eight ideas are simple ones to read or to recite. The living of them may be your foundation for mature self-regulation of the remaining parts of your life's time line. As with many of the prescriptions for effectiveness in living, lip service is easy. Actual doing of these things and the experiencing of their effects is your challenge and the essence of *Self Actualization*.

Idea 1. Wholeness

Each person is each person. Your total configuration is a unity rather than an collection of parts, each owned by some central command center. If you lose a finger, an appendix, a leg, or have a stroke, then you become a new configuration rather than remaining the old configuration minus parts. The fantasy insistence upon remaining as you were before change occurred is at the core of existential pain and accounts <u>for</u> much extended misery.

Thus one does not *have* parts of one's person. This business of *having* has confused human affairs for all of our history by creating a reversed formula for life style which begins with *possession:*

_____*"If I only had the right job, I could do what I want and finally be the person I'd like to be."* With the **wholeness** approach that formula is returned to it's inevitable sequence:

"I *am* all that I am and out of that I *do* what I do and then I *have* whatever results come from my *being* and *doing*!

PEAK points:

Formula one: Have – Do – Be = Partial Person.

Formula two: Be – Do – Have = Whole person.

Idea 2: Contextuality:

All life occurs within some matrix. The interaction between the life and the matrix leads to definition and meaning. This may appear to be conflicting with idea 1 because it implies that your wholeness does not end at your skin but includes contact and exchanges with the environment. Yet the archetypal stories highlight the human drama by showing that heroes in one context become villains in different contexts. The admired sedentary behavior of the intellectual in one's library becomes absurd on the Lumberjack trial.

The effective life style is accountable for the interaction between you and your environment. Since the outside world's realities are in constant flux and therefore perturbing, many people attempt to cope by refusing to notice or act upon not-preferred parts of the environmental pageant. Some operate on the theory that if they will hold themselves constant the environment will become constant.

A fully functioning life style is in contact and making responsible exchanges with the environmental flow – satisfying deficits and eliminating surpluses. This is often not easy as contexts change and alter one's position in life. The astronaut returned from space is an ex-astronaut. The president defeated becomes a different person and the reverse-(the suddenly powerful common candidate). We are indeed humbled to consider how easily the integrity of one's identity/context are tampered with by the flummery of environmental events.

PEAK Points:

Same self – same world = Catatonia.

Same self – changing world = Stubbornness.

Changing world – Changing self = Coping.

Changing world – *Choosing* self = Health.74

Idea 3: Proactivity:

Early in life most of us learn of the horror and embarrassment that comes with making mistakes. The lessons are heavy enough that we learn not to be impulsive. We learn to sit back and see what develops before doing anything and regard ourselves as re-actors.

But the social reality is that people do things and things do get done by people. The nasty part is that much of the boring unpleasant task activity is assigned by the pro-actors to be done by the re-actors. Thus the economic and political systems are born and become complex. In the Grown Up view of things however, your capacity for pro-acivity is constantly ready despite having been habitually deferred. The excitements of being alive rather than zombie-like are centered around the pro-active awareness that you do, in fact, select every one of your responses to all events. Habits often preclude awareness of these selections and how they are made and this accounts for how we are programmed. In the mature perspective there are no programs which are immune to reactivated awareness revision and resourcefulness.

PEAK POINTS: You select the style menu:

REACT	PROACT
Watch out!	Observe.
Don't make mistakes	Learn from errors.
Wait and see.	Do something.
Take what's left.	Go for what's important.
Habit.	Choice.
Being "done to".	Doing.

1dea 4. Awareness:

You have several modes of awareness capability. They include sensing, emoting, knowing, and thinking. These modes begin with sensory perception of external information and proprioception (internal body sensations). Examples of sensory disadvantaged people like Helen Keller and Steve Wonder provide evidence of the remarkable capacity of the human organism to fulfill its sensoric trust and provide life with the full excitements of sound, touch, balance, and satiation.

Emotional life is constant and ranges from sorrow and terror through boredom and beyond to ecstasy and joy. The movement variable is also a constant life force although much of it may be censored out of awareness. Movement is continuous and multi-dimensional in all living organisms and is dynamic as well. Movement not only results from

107

immediate sensory, emotional, and cognitive stimuli, it also has the power to induce them. For example: movement in the walls of your intestine, of which you are typically unaware, will likely result in some sensation of urgency within the next three hours. If the food supply is depleted, or the bathroom is occupied when it comes your time – a complex of intra/inter-personal emotional and cognitive events will be set in motion. *Thinking* is the mode of awareness most easily admired and criticized. Our ability to think has done wonderful things for the benefit of all of us. It has also brought us to our terrors of one another. *Thinking* is done by remembering and by creating new patterns from existing symbols, or by mixing memories and intentions to make plans or hopes. You *Think* by activating sensory modes to organize information from the world or mobilizing it from within. You make pictures, use language, hear sounds, notice body urges and sensations as well as smells and tastes.

The development of Neuro-Linguistic Programming (NLP) has emphasized the notion that each of you relies preferentially on one of the above modalities to make meaning from information received. The preference may change across different contexts, but there appears to be a primary reliance on one modality in any given circumstance. Following this model, there is an exciting potential for understanding mis-communications! If the sender is operating from one preferred mode and the receiver is operating in a different one, the message process will suffer.

A second exciting potential emerges as the NLP modelers (Bandler and Grinder 1975-79) have observed that skillful communicators demonstrate flexibility among the modalities and consistently match the preferences of those with whom they are interacting. Still a third excitement emerges as we consider internal processes from Gestalt Therapy: The Top Dog messages tend to be formed from visual and auditory references while the Under Dog tends to operate from body feelings as the referent. Awareness systems, thus formed, often do not integrate well until each system accepts information from the other's preferred modality. BARKING becomes the exchange mode.

Peak Points: CHOICE rests on Awareness

See, hear, feel – NOW

See, hear, feel – Remember

See, hear, feel – Create

See, hear, feel – Match

Idea 5 Response-ability:

Before Genesis was written we wanted to find ways to locate responsibility for the human condition outside of ourselves. If not The Creator, the apple, the snake, or the woman, it was not **_Me_** to blame. We have used religion, government, enemies, ancestors, parents, spouses, children, schooling, geography, climate, ownership of the means of production, health conditions, and a glory of episodes to explain or justify ourselves and our choices.

Such sands are running out. Each of us is *Response-Able*. Every person must actually do or misdo his or her style and living choices. You are response-able and responsible for all covert and overt behavioral and thought choices. **I can't help it !** is obsolete as a life style or explanation. The buck doesn't stop with Harry Truman or George W. Bush –

Each of us has our own buck.

PEAK points:

If you keep doing what you have been doing, you'll keep getting the same results..

If what you did didn't work, do something different.

If you don't like what is happening, take *response ability* to:

A Change First!

B. Act as if the *healing* process is already under way.

C. Appreciate small steps and small improvements.

D. Do the required or appropriate behavior even if you don't feel like doing it.

Idea 6. Resourcefulness:

When *Laziness* competes with *Creativeness*, the odds are even a great deal of the time.

The womb was a great place with automatic resources. Many recover from it haltingly if at all. Much of the cunning in human life runs toward creating artificial replacement wombs such as enough wealth to yield adequate investment income, or surrounding one's self with loyal and unquestioning companions. The idea is to get to the point where environmental support is automatic and secure. Further effort would not be required. When these conditions prevail, the excitements of living become vulnerable to automation. *Effort* may become obsolete and *boredom* can become the major feature of the *Now*. The enjoyments of retirement can thus be pre-empted. We see that many such retirees resume careers or just go to work to occupy the stream of time facing them.

The functioning *life style* is focused upon the mobilization and application of resources and assets. The outlook is that each of us is endowed with everything needed to live effectively and to make restoration when damages have occurred in our lives.

You direct your life through each moment by using your sensory equipment to be aware of your self and your environment to make choices as events unfold. When you rely upon habit or obsolete beliefs you deaden your own creativity. You become lazy and return to the *I can't help it style*. (Review chapter four; Activating Rsources). When you Mobilize your resources, strengths, and assets you are infused with vitality and become a real person – one who makes *being in a couple* fulfilling and wothwhile for both you and your partner.

Idea 7 Existentiality:

__Being__ is our lot until we *Be* no more. Then we will only have been and the future will include only what our *Beings* have yielded. So while we have the chance, we are behooved to do it well. This is sobering. We humans have an affinity for both predictions and traditions and a plethora of *FAITHS* for the enigmas of death and time.

Five thousand years ago the Scribes wrote about the end of life and the end of the world as well as the beginnings. Without beginnings and endings, our attachments waver. Time becomes the foe that must submit to measurement. Your **Now** remains the moment of aliveness and direct experience can be done only in the now.

In many contemporary therapeutic perspectives all time is treated in the present. Dr. Frederick Perls et.al., (1976) formed a revealing style with this time dimension. Instead of permitting patients to fantasize about the future or recall the past, he showed them how to bring either dimension into the <u>**NOW**</u> and to go beyond remembering or predicting into direct re-experiencing. We don't travel forward or backward through time. Rather, we remain always flowing in the now and bring experiences from the *There and Then* into the *Here and Now.*

Recent developments in <u>*Time-line Therapy*</u> (James et.al., 1989)_ revise the movement component by creating metaphorical structures of time, usually in the form of linear modes. A typical mode would have the *past* located in a line that extends behind one's self backward into birth or beyond, while the *future* extends forward and inclines upward. (See <u>*Your Timelines,*</u> Chapter four). With this approach, once a congruent structure of your time line has been identified, you may easily visualize floating above it to locate and inspect any events which may profit from further examination or re-structuring (James & Woodsmall 1989). While *Hind Sight* may be 20/20, *Present Sight* provides analytical review of choice points and their outcomes. You can **PEAK** yourself to improved potentials for choice making the next time.

PEAK points:

The PAST is done.	NOW is for sure.	The FUTURE is not here yet.
	Here is where you can:	
	Take stock	
	Make choices	
	Decide	
	Experience results	
	Do things (be-do-have)	
	Plan,	
	Design,	
	Invent.	
	Prepare	
	Practice	
	Be responsible	
	Live!	

<u>Idea 8 The Naturalness Of Persons:</u>

Stories have always helped us as we have struggled with being persons. One problem is that most stories have plots with good guys and bad guys. Many of us operate under the assumption that there is one vast cosmic story replete with plot, heroes, villains and the "silent moral/ immoral majorities". The enlightened view regards this as an absurd assumption and further removes the stigma of character value from persons. Every person is exactly that – a person: neither intrinsically good nor intrinsically bad. We all choose constantly and sometimes the behaviors or decisions are bad choices, but even a bad choice maker remains - a person. When anyone steps beyond established roles the plot changes for better or worse.

As you have grown up, the business of dropping your roles in order to meet life as a person has often been challenging. In your couple relationship, your roles become locked in place. When you step out of any of your roles, the script becomes dysfunctional. Without the script, you face an existential emptiness. It effects both partners. Facing this vacuum is scary and locates the moments of truth right within the immediate aware center of each person. Persons, not actors, must re-write the script. The time will have come to re-invent who you are with each other. That's quite a task for anyone who has been a pawn for The Great Playwrite in the Sky for a number of years. (See Chapter Seven: Platforms for Negotiating). Peak well!

<u>Peak points:</u>

Eight ideas to either recite or to live:

Wholeness	Response-ablitiy
Contextuality	Resourcefulness
Proactivity	Existentiality
Awareness	Naturalness of persons

Since 1954, in teaching and practicing Counseling Concepts, these ideas in various combinations have shown themselves to be present and active in people who recover from emotional stress and return to wholesomeness and emotional health.

I have come to believe that most of us are a bit fearful about growing up completely. Those who appear to do so will ably demonstrate versions of these ideas with consistency. They are among the Keys for a wholesome, compassionate, playful, and mature life.

Ever onward, RES 2003

Reference List

Andreas,C. & Andreas,S. 1987 *Change Your mind-And Keep the Change*. Moab, Utah: Real People Press.

------------------------------1889 *Heart of the Mind*. Moab, Utah: Real People Press.

Andreas, C. & Andreas,T. 1994 *Core Transformation*. Moab, Utah: Real People Press.

Bandler, R. and Grinder,J. 1975 *The Structure of Magic.*vols. I & II. PaloAlto: Science and Behavior Books

Cameron-Bandler, L. 1985 *Solutions*. Moab Utah: Real People Press.

------------------------- 1985 *The Emprint Method*. San Rafeal, CA: Future Pace, Inc.

------------------------- 1985 *Know How*. San Rafael, CA: Future Pace, Inc.

Dilts, R, et.al. 1980 *Neuro-Linguist Programming,Volume 1*. Cupertino, CA.: Meta Publications.

Fisher.R. and Ury, W. 1981*Getting To Yes*. Bergenfield, NJ: Penguin Press

Fisher, R. and Brown, R. 1988 *Getting Together*. Boston: Houghton Mifflin.

Frankl, V.E. 1963 *Man's Search For Meaning*. New York: Beacon Press.

Guerney, B. G. Jr. 1977 *Relationship Enhancement*. San Francisco; Jossey-Bass, Inc.

James, T & Woodsmall, W. 1988 Time Line Therapy

Koch, Joanne, 1976 *The Marriage Savers*. Toronto: Longman Canada Limited.

Maslow, A. H. 1962 *Toward a Psychology of Being*. Princeton, New Jersey; D. Van Nostrand Co.

McGraw, P.C. 2000 *Relationship Rescue*. New York; Hyperion.

Perls, F. 1976 *The Growing Edge of Gestalt Therapy*. New York: Bruner/Maxel.

Polster, E. & Polster, M. 1973 *Gestalt Therapy Integrated*. New York: Brunner/Maxel

Rogers, C. 1961 *On Becoming A Person*. Boston: Houghton Mifflin.

Tannen, D. 1998 *The Argument Culture*. New York: Random House.

Zinker, J. 1977.*Creative Process in Gestalt Therapy*. New York; Bruner/Mazel

About The Author

Robert E. Saltmarsh ED.D. is usually called Bob or Salty. He is retired from Eastern Illinois University Since 1997 when he completed his tour as Chair Person of the Department of Counseling and Student Development. He initiated efforts to achieve what are now fully accredited Master of Sc. and Master of Ed. Degree programs in both Community and School Counseling. These programs lead to Licensure and or Certification in these fields.

Bob began his career as a High School Teacher and Head Football Coach in Ohio (1954). His talents as a Counselor emerged quickly as demanded by the class room and the locker room. Completion of Master's Degree (Miami (O) 1964) and Doctorate (Indiana University 1969) led to Faculty Status at Eastern Illinois University in 1969 as a Teacher and Counselor Educator.

Believing that teaching others about counseling is best supported by doing counseling one's self, Bob established a part time private practice which endures today. His professional, academic, and anecdotal contributions have appeared in journals, regional media, and local publications. Presentations at National, State, and Private Conventions and Workshops have been well received. Prior to retirement, such presentations averaged 20 to 30 per academic year.

The BARK & PEAK Models were developed and clarified during the 43 years of Salty's personal and professional adventures.

Salty and wife -- Markay are pleased that retirement is indeed a gift.